The Lord is My Shepherd

For Ben

Text copyright © 2004 by Christopher L. Webber
Illustrations copyright © 2004 by Preston McDaniels

Morehouse Publishing   Morehouse Publishing
P.O. Box 1321   The Tower Building
Harrisburg, PA 17105   11 York Road, London SE1 7NX

Morehouse Publishing is a Continuum imprint.

Design by Trude Brummer

Library of Congress Cataloging-in-Publication Data

Webber, Christopher.
  The Lord is my shepherd : Psalm 23 for children / retold by
Christopher L. Webber ; illustrated by Preston McDaniels.
     p. cm. — (Psalms for children)
  ISBN 0-8192-1986-X (hardcover)
  1. Bible. O.T. Psalms XXIII—Paraphrases, English—Juvenile
literature. [1. Bible. O.T. Psalms XXIII—Paraphrases.] I. McDaniels,
Preston, ill. II. Title.
  BS145023rd .W43 2004
  223'.209505—dc22

                         2003025302

Printed in Malaysia

04 05 06 07 08 09   10 9 8 7 6 5 4 3 2 1

The Lord is My Shepherd

Psalm 23 for Children

Retold by

Christopher L. Webber

Illustrated by

Preston McDaniels

MOREHOUSE PUBLISHING
A Continuum imprint
HARRISBURG • LONDON • NEW YORK

*T*he Lord is my shepherd
who gives me all I need.

My shepherd lets me rest
on the green grass

And leads me beside peaceful streams of water.

When I'm tired, the Lord makes me feel strong again
and shows me the right path to follow.
The Lord never breaks a promise.

Even when I am sad and everything looks dark
I will never have to be afraid

*B*ecause my shepherd walks beside me
and carries a staff to protect me.

*L*ord, you set out a feast for me to share
and protect me while I eat.

You treat me like a special guest.

You fill my cup to the brim.

*T*he goodness and love of God will come
to me every day of my life.
and God will be with me forever.

Christopher L. Webber is the author of over a dozen books, and his hymns appear in several major hymnals. He has ministered to inner-city, suburban, and overseas parishes, and he currently serves two small congregations in rural northwestern Connecticut. He has been married for over 40 years to Margaret Elisabeth Webber; they have four grown children and three grandchildren.

Photo by Hal Maggiore

Preston McDaniels' interest in art began as a young child when he entertained himself by drawing. He also fell in love with music as a child, and still plays his trusty piano each morning. He combined his love of music and his talent for illustration in four critically acclaimed books of hymns for children, *God of the Sparrow, All Things Bright and Beautiful, Earth & All Stars*, and *Now the Day Is Over*, all available from Morehouse Publishing. He lives in Nebraska with his wife, Cindy, and two daughters, Abby and Lizzie.